Sensei Self Development

Mental Health Chronicles Series

Learning to Accept Yourself and Your Life Experience

Sensei Paul David

Copyright Page

Sensei Self Development -
Learning to Accept Yourself and Your Life Experience,
by Sensei Paul David

Copyright © 2024

SENSEI PUBLISHING

It's A Great Day To Be Alive!

www.senseipublishing.com

@senseipublishing
senseipublishing

Get/Share Your FREE SSD Mental Health Chronicles at
www.senseiselfdevelopment.care

or

CLICK HERE

Check Out The SSD Chronicles Series CLICK HERE

Dedication

To those who courageously take action
towards self-improvement - you are helping to
evolve the world for generations to come.

- It's a great day to be alive!

If Found Please Contact:

_____

Reward If Found:

_____

MY
COMMITMENT

I, _____

commit to writing This Sensei Self
Development Journal for at least 10 days in a
row, starting: _____

Writing this journal is valuable to me because:

_____

_____

_____

_____

_____

_____

If I finish a minimum of 10 consecutive days of
writing in this journal, I will reward myself by:

_____

_____

_____

_____

_____

_____

If I don't finish 10 days of writing this journal, I will promise to:

_____

_____

_____

_____

_____

_____

I will do the following things to ensure that I write in my Sensei Self Development Journal every day:

_____

_____

_____

_____

_____

_____

Get/Share Your FREE All-Ages Mental Health eBook Now at

www.senseiselfdevelopment.com

Or CLICK HERE

senseiselfdevelopment.com

Check Out Another Book In The
SSD BOOK SERIES:

senseipublishing.com/SSD_SERIES

CLICK HERE

Join Our Publishing Journey!

If you would like to receive FUTURE FREE BOOKS and get to know us better, please click www.senseipublishing.com and join our newsletter by entering your email address in the pop-up box.

Follow Our Blog: senseipauldavid.ca

Follow/Like/Subscribe: Facebook, Instagram, YouTube: @senseipublishing

Scan the QR Code with your phone or tablet

to follow us on social media: Like / Subscribe / Follow

A Message From The Author:
Sensei Paul David

Dear Reader,

Welcome to the world of mental health journaling – a sacred space for self-reflection, growth, and healing. Within these pages, you hold the power to uplift your spirit, invigorate your mind, and nourish your goals.

In a world that often moves at blink-and-you'll-miss-it speed, it's crucial to make time for self-care and self-discovery.

Anxiety, stress, and emotional turbulence may have clouded your mind, making it difficult to find clarity and peace within. But fear not! Together, we will navigate the labyrinth of emotions, and experiences, helping to simplify the path to mental well-being.

This journal is not merely a bunch of blank pages awaiting your words. It is your compassionate companion, offering solace and understanding during your unique journey. Here, you are free to unburden yourself, celebrate small and large victories, and confront the challenges that may still linger.

Within the sheltered realm of these pages, there is no judgment, no expectation, and no pressure. Your unique experience and perspective hold immeasurable worth, and your voice deserves to be heard. Whether you choose to fill the lines with eloquence or simply scribble fragments of your thoughts, please remember each entry is a valuable contribution to your growth.

In this sacred space, you are challenged to take off the mask we so often wear in the outside world. It is here that you can be raw, vulnerable, and authentic – allowing your true self to be seen and embraced without reservation. By giving yourself permission to explore the depths of your emotions and confront the shadows that may lurk within, you will discover profound insights and find the healing you seek over time.

As you embark on this journaling journey, I encourage you to embrace the process itself rather than fixate solely on the outcome. Remember, it is not about reaching a certain destination or ticking off boxes on a list of accomplishments. Rather, it is about cultivating self-awareness, fostering self-compassion, and nurturing a sense of curiosity about the intricate workings of your intelligently beautiful mind.

In the quiet moments of reflection, let your pen become a bridge between your inner world and the possibilities that lie ahead. Create a sanctuary for your thoughts, fears, triumphs, and dreams. As you pour your heart onto these pages, allow your words to be a living testament to courage, resilience, and an unwavering commitment to your own well-being.

I am honored to be a part of your journey, and I believe in your ability to navigate the twists and turns with grace and resilience. Remember, you are not alone in this – countless others have walked similar paths, faced similar challenges, and emerged stronger and wiser on the other side. You have the power to reclaim all of your untapped joy, cultivate a positive mindset that serves you, and foster a deep sense of self-love and peaceful confident. – And it will take a worth effort and time.

So, open the first page of this journal with hope, curiosity, and an open heart and open mind. Embrace the transformative power of self-reflection, and allow it to guide you towards a life of greater fulfilment and peace. Each journaling session is an opportunity to not only connect with yourself but also to rekindle the light within that sometimes flickers but never extinguishes.

Remember, the pages you are about to fill are not just a record of your journey but also a testament to your strength, resilience, and indomitable spirit. Cherish this space, invest in yourself, and let your words be an ode to the magnificent journey of becoming whole.

With great respect for your decision to evolve,

Paul

MY CONVICTION

Please circle your answers below

I am DECIDING to be patient with myself and this PROCESS each time I journal toward my improved state of mental well-being

YES   NO

"The present moment is filled with joy and happiness. If you are attentive, you will see it."

Thich Nhat Hanh

Introduction

When asked to describe myself, I usually mention a variety of things. I could tell you I'm a teacher, a writer, talk about my daily habits, my appearance, my family, or even the town I live in now or where I grew up. Typically, these details paint a picture of who I am. But there are times when I think in a completely different way. Instead of who I am, I ponder about who I could have been. I think about alternate paths my life might have taken, different versions of myself that could have existed if certain events in my past had played out differently. We all could probably create such a list - like if I had chosen a different college, or not taken that specific class with that particular teacher. What if my girlfriend hadn't broken up with me, or my parents hadn't divorced, or if I had chosen a different job, or if my circumstances with my partner had been different?... what would I be like?

There's an endless number of lives I'm not living, so why do certain unchosen paths bother me more than others? Why does it matter to me that I'm not living a particular life? It doesn't bother me that I'm not a podiatrist or a landscape designer, that I can't play the flute. I don't dwell on not living in Birmingham. These aren't the things that stir my soul. But the fact that I'm not as generous as my wife, as intelligent as my friend, or as humorous as my brother; that I'm no longer young as I was... these thoughts are constant companions. They're with me when I leave the house.

By telling you what I'm not, I'm also revealing who I am.

I remember standing on a wet sidewalk, slumped, as a bus pulled away. It carried a version of me who hadn't stopped to remove a pebble from his shoe at Macy's. This other me sat comfortably on the bus, taking out his phone and fitting in his earbuds. But as the bus turned the corner, he disappeared. Yet, I don't need a dry, untroubled alter ego to know I'm impatient and dislike being caught in the rain. Sometimes, though, my imagined selves linger longer and reveal more about me.

For some, the thought of unexperienced lives can be distressing, even leading to a personal crisis. Take the story of Spencer Brydon from Henry James's "The Jolly Corner". Brydon, in his youth, left America for Europe to live a life of indulgence. Returning to New York thirty years later, he sees his friends who have become wealthy, influential, and established. Single and with only superficial achievements,

Brydon starts to question what would have happened if he had stayed in America. Could he have been as rich as them? Would he have married his friend Alice, whom he has recently reconnected with? He obsessively roams his childhood home at night, haunted by the idea that the ghost of his potential self lingers there. This leads to a chilling encounter with an apparitional version of himself – a menacing figure missing two fingers. This experience causes Brydon to faint, and he wakes up in Alice's care, realizing his love for her and preferring his current life over the alternative.

Most of us don't experience such intense haunting by our potential selves. Yet, there are moments or periods when we sense that things could have been different. David Byrne's lyrics in the Talking Heads' song "Once in a Lifetime" capture this sentiment: "You may find yourself in a beautiful house, with a beautiful wife," and then question, "Well, how did I get here?" You might feel overwhelmed by life, wondering if you could have shaped it differently. You might recall, as Hilary Mantel did, a version of yourself that exists only as a nascent thought, like an unfinished story. There are days when your life feels uncomfortable, a constant reminder of its presence. Byrne's lyrics continue, "You may tell yourself, 'This is not my beautiful house... This is not my beautiful wife.'"

Why do we think like that?

Our contemplation of the roads not taken might reflect our modern lifestyle. Unled lives are a largely modern preoccupation. Traditionally, people often lived lives similar to their parents or followed a path dictated by fate. In contrast, today we seek to navigate our own paths. In the Iliad, Achilles faces two predestined choices set by the gods: a heroic death at Troy or a long, unremarkable life. He ultimately chooses battle. Our contemporary world, however, isn't as straightforward. Achilles didn't grapple with decisions like choosing a career path in medicine or law. In our world, such choices are significant, with the understanding that they can shape our entire lives.

For those who don't believe in an afterlife, the significance of this one life is magnified. Adam Phillips, a psychologist, explores this in his book "Missing Out: In Praise of the Unlived Life." He cautions that when our hopes for a better, more fulfilling life are confined to this one, we face a significant challenge. With only one chance at existence, the pressure is on not just to live, but to live well.

This perspective often leads us to view our life story as a narrative of missed opportunities and paths not taken.

In today's capitalist society, where individualism reigns supreme and choices multiply rapidly, we're confronted with an ever-increasing array of paths not taken. This culture prizes choice as a paramount good and often sees randomness as an unwelcome surprise. We're constantly making decisions, exciting yet overwhelming, and we habitually review our past to better navigate the future. This mindset fuels our sense of the unfulfilled potential selves. Advertisers play into this by tempting us with visions of improved versions of ourselves, capitalizing on the 'you only live once' (YOLO) philosophy mixed with a fear of missing out (FOMO). Furthermore, the structure of our work life deepens this sentiment. Today's career landscape, unlike the more straightforward agricultural or industrial past, is filled with specialized roles and achievement ladders. With each career choice, we inherently forego other possibilities. As we climb our chosen ladder, there's a tendency to reflect on the rungs we never stepped on.

Jean-Paul Sartre spoke about the allure of imaginary lives, "A man commits himself and draws his own portrait, outside of which there is nothing." While this perspective might seem stark, it suggests that the tangible reality is what truly counts. In Sartre's view, dreams, expectations, and hopes end up defining a person as a collection of unfulfilled desires and missed opportunities.

Sartre's philosophy emphasized the importance of focusing on our actual deeds and future endeavors, rather than dwelling on hypotheticals or what-ifs. He noted that people often undervalue the extent of their actions. He asserted that an artist should not be defined solely by their artistic works, as many other elements also shape who they are. We generally achieve more than we realize; our real lives are often richer than we give them credit for. This is why keeping a diary can be beneficial, as it allows us to see and appreciate the fullness of the lives we actually live.

The thoughts of what we could have, should have, or would have done follow a logical pattern of 'if-then' scenarios. Yet, we are often captivated by alternate versions of ourselves that barely make logical sense. Consider the musician Melissa Etheridge, who, when deciding to have children with her partner, had to choose between two friends as the sperm donor: David Crosby or Brad Pitt. They ultimately chose Crosby. Etheridge humorously remarked later that her teenagers mused, "I could have had Brad Pitt as a father. I could've been amazingly handsome." This brings to mind a joke about a man named Lev: "If I were the Czar, I would be richer than the Czar," he claims to a friend. Puzzled, his friend asks how that could be. Lev replies, "If I were the Czar, I'd teach Hebrew lessons on the side." These scenarios raise the question: If I'm the Czar or Brad Pitt's son, am I still myself? The notion that I could also be someone else seems to find a loophole in language, forming a sentence that doesn't quite make logical sense. Yet, perhaps it's this very senselessness, the wish to be someone else, that attracts us. We long for a world that's more fluid and radiant than the one we inhabit.

How to Accept Your Life's Experiences

Understand How Happiness Works

In "Stumbling on Happiness," Daniel Gilbert explores the complex nature of happiness and how our predictions about what will make us happy are often inaccurate. One key takeaway from his research is that our expectations about future happiness are frequently misguided. We tend to overestimate the impact that major life events, both good and bad, will have on our happiness.

For example, we might think that achieving a particular career milestone, acquiring a new possession, or even changing a life path will bring us great happiness. However, research suggests that these events might not have as long-lasting or as intense an impact on our happiness as we anticipate. Similarly, we might fear that certain misfortunes or missed opportunities will bring us great unhappiness, but in reality, their impact is often less severe and more transient than we expect.

This phenomenon occurs partly because of our brain's ability to adapt to new situations – a process known as hedonic adaptation. We quickly get used to changes in our circumstances, whether positive or negative, and return to a baseline level of happiness.

Gilbert's work also highlights the importance of more mundane, everyday sources of happiness that we often overlook. Strong social connections, a sense of community, engaging in fulfilling activities, and having a sense of purpose are consistently linked to long-term happiness. These aspects of life tend to bring more sustained satisfaction than the pursuit of extraordinary achievements or material possessions.

The implication of this understanding is significant when contemplating life's choices and paths not taken. It suggests that the alternate lives we fantasize about might not be as fulfilling as we imagine, and that our current life, with its everyday joys and connections, may already contain many of the key ingredients for happiness. This perspective can encourage a greater appreciation for the present and a reevaluation of what truly matters in the pursuit of a happy and meaningful life.

Mindfulness

Mindfulness is about living in the present moment and accepting it as it is. This means noticing your thoughts, feelings, and bodily sensations without trying to change or judge them. By practicing mindfulness, you become more aware of the reality of your current experiences, reducing the focus on hypothetical "what-ifs" or alternate realities.

When you're mindful, you acknowledge and accept your thoughts and emotions. This can be especially helpful when you find yourself dwelling on paths not taken or imagining different versions of your life. Mindfulness helps you see these thoughts for what they are – just thoughts, not definitive truths about your life or your identity.

Practicing mindfulness can be as simple as taking a few moments to focus on your breathing, going for a mindful walk, or even engaging in daily activities with full attention. These practices help ground you in the here and now and discredit your thoughts as not something you truly desire but as temporary apparition into your consciousness. Thoughts arise spontaneously and are often influenced by past experiences and external factors. Recognizing this can help you to not over-identify with your thoughts, especially when they are negative or unhelpful.

Common Humanity

The concept of common humanity centers around the idea that everyone shares similar experiences, emotions, and challenges in life. It's the understanding that no one is alone in their journey, and the experiences that we often view as uniquely ours are, in fact, part of the broader human experience.

So, not just you, but everyone else, the rich, the famous, contemplate on what their life could have been if they had picked a different spouse, spent more time with their family, or had a different approach to life. Michael Jackson, for instance, longed for his lost childhood.

This realization can be particularly comforting when reflecting on life's choices and the feelings of isolation that might come from wondering about different paths.

When you consider the various turns your life has taken, remembering our common humanity can put your experiences in perspective. It highlights that the doubts, joys, and uncertainties you face are shared by many. This shared experience can foster a sense of connectedness and empathy, not just towards others, but also towards yourself.

Recognizing common humanity encourages a kinder, more compassionate approach to life. It helps in dealing with personal challenges by reminding you that struggles and setbacks are not failures, but part of what it means to be human. This perspective promotes a more forgiving and understanding attitude towards yourself and your life story. Yes, things could have been better, but things could have been much worse as well. And as we know hell goes much much deeper.

In embracing the shared nature of human experiences, you can find comfort in knowing that your journey, with all its unique aspects, is also a part of a larger, collective human narrative. This understanding can lead to a deeper acceptance of life as it is, recognizing that each experience, whether perceived as good or bad, is a part of what connects us all in the human experience.

Gratitude

Gratitude, the act of recognizing and appreciating the positive aspects of life, is a powerful tool for accepting life's experiences. It shifts the focus from what's missing or what could have been, to what's present and valuable in your life. This shift can significantly impact your overall well-being and perspective.

When practicing gratitude, you actively acknowledge the good in your life, which can be as simple as appreciating a sunny day, the comfort of a friend, or even your own abilities and accomplishments. This practice encourages a positive mindset, even in challenging situations. For instance, if you're dealing with a difficult job situation, gratitude can help you appreciate the aspects of your job that are fulfilling or the skills you've gained.

Keeping a gratitude journal is a popular and effective way to cultivate this mindset.

Regularly writing down things you're grateful for can train your brain to notice and appreciate the positive.

Practicing gratitude also fosters resilience. When faced with tough situations, focusing on what you're grateful for can provide a sense of stability and hope. It helps in recognizing that even in hard times, there are aspects of life that are positive and worth valuing.

Self Compassion

Self-compassion is a fundamental aspect of accepting life's experiences and is particularly effective in dealing with thoughts about paths not taken or potential selves. Self-compassion involves treating oneself with the same kindness, concern, and understanding that one would show to a good friend. It has three main components:

1. Self-kindness vs. Self-judgment: This involves being understanding and kind to oneself in instances of pain or failure, rather

than being harshly self-critical. For example, if you're ruminating over a missed opportunity or a path not taken, self-kindness would involve recognizing that making mistakes or facing setbacks is a part of being human and doesn't define your worth.

2. Common Humanity vs. Isolation: This component emphasizes that suffering and personal inadequacy are part of the shared human experience. It's about recognizing that you're not alone in your struggles. When you think about what you haven't achieved or paths you didn't take, it's helpful to remember that everyone has similar feelings and experiences.

3. Mindfulness vs. Over-Identification: Mindfulness in self-compassion involves a balanced approach to negative emotions so that feelings are neither suppressed nor exaggerated. It allows you to hold your thoughts and feelings about unfulfilled paths in mindful awareness, recognizing them as valid but not letting them define you.

Practicing self-compassion can be done through exercises like writing a letter to yourself from a compassionate friend's perspective, or by speaking to yourself in a kind and understanding voice. It's about actively soothing and comforting yourself in times of distress, and reminding yourself of your common humanity to reduce feelings of isolation.

By practicing self-compassion, you can learn to accept life as it is, with all its imperfections, and treat yourself with the same kindness you would offer to others. This approach leads to greater emotional resilience, lower levels of anxiety and depression, and a more positive state of mind.

Self Esteem

Self-esteem directly influences how you perceive and navigate your life's journey. It's a reflection of how much you value and trust yourself. With a strong sense of self-esteem, you're more likely to view the choices you've made, including those that led you away from certain paths, in a positive light. You understand that each decision has contributed to your growth and has its own value.

For instance, if you chose a career that's different from what you once dreamed, high self-esteem helps you see the strengths and skills you've gained, rather than just mourning the lost dream.

Healthy self-esteem also plays a crucial role in how you face life's uncertainties and challenges. It gives you the confidence to take risks and step out of your comfort zone, knowing that your worth isn't solely defined by outcomes or achievements. This confidence can lead to a more fulfilling and authentic life, where decisions are driven by your true self, not by fear or the need for approval.

In everyday life, self-esteem manifests in the way you handle setbacks, interact with others, and pursue your goals. It's about having a balanced view of yourself, acknowledging your strengths, and accepting your limitations without self-criticism. High self-esteem doesn't mean you won't have regrets or wonder about other possibilities, but it does mean you won't let these thoughts undermine your sense of self or your current path.

Trust Thyself

Trust yourself. Rely on your own instincts, judgments, and beliefs. It's an affirmation that you have the wisdom and strength within yourself to make the right choices for your life. This trust is about listening to your inner voice and honoring it, even when it goes against external pressures or opinions.

When you trust yourself, you navigate life's decisions with a sense of personal integrity. This doesn't mean you'll always make perfect choices, but it does mean you're making choices that are true to who you are. For instance, if you're at a crossroads in your career, trusting yourself means choosing a path that aligns with your values and aspirations, not just what is expected or traditional.

This self-trust also helps when reflecting on past decisions and paths not taken. It allows you to view these moments with understanding and acceptance, knowing that they were the best decisions for you at that time, based on what you knew and felt.

In daily life, trusting yourself can manifest in various ways: standing up for your beliefs, pursuing a passion that others might not understand, or even admitting when you need help. It's a fundamental belief in your own abilities and worth, and it guides you through life's ups and downs with a sense of confidence and authenticity.

Embrace Vulnerability

When you allow yourself to be vulnerable, you open up to more authentic experiences. You learn to accept and embrace your life as it is, not as you think it should be. This can lead to deeper connections with others and a greater sense of fulfillment.

Embracing vulnerability means acknowledging your feelings about these choices without judgment. It's understanding that it's natural to have regrets or to wonder about what could have been, but also knowing that these feelings don't define your entire life.

Embracing vulnerability is not about weakness; it's about courage and strength. It takes bravery to face the unknown and to be open about your true self. This approach can lead to a richer, more authentic life experience.

Cultivate Respect

Having respect for yourself, your life, and the people in it, essentially means embracing where you are without longing to be someone else. It's a recognition that changing your identity or circumstances wouldn't necessarily lead to a better life, because it would mean not being 'you.' It's about confidence in your own path and worth, understanding that your life, with its unique blend of challenges and joys, is valid and valuable.

This viewpoint dismisses the notion that someone else's life is inherently better. Sure, others might excel in certain areas or possess attributes you don't, but this doesn't diminish your own worth. Self-respect is about understanding that these comparisons are superficial and that true worth comes from within.

It's crucial to remember that wishing for a different life is like wishing away your own existence.

When you have respect for yourself, you don't want to be someone else because it is disrespectful to YOU. There should be no man or woman alive you think is inherently more deserving or better than you. I don't care who it is. It's okay to look up to someone, but not want to be someone.

Before We Get Started…

Remember, mindfulness journaling is a personal practice, and these questions are meant to guide and inspire you. Feel free to adapt and modify them to suit your needs and preferences. Explore, reflect, and embrace the opportunity to deepen your self-awareness and cultivate a sense of inner peace.

Date ___ / ___ / ___ : S   M   T   W   Th   F   S

I feel:
(please circle)

because   because   because   because   because

_____ _____ _____ _____ _____

_____ _____ _____ _____ _____

Today I Am Grateful For

1. _____

2. _____

3. _____

What could help transform today into a remarkable day?

Reflective Writing

How have you benefitted from the process of learning to accept yourself and your life experience?

_____

_____

_____

_____

_____

_____

_____

Which of the following is not a key component of self-acceptance?

a) Acknowledging your strengths and weaknesses
b) Comparing yourself to others
c) Practicing self-compassion
d) Embracing your flaws and imperfections

All Are Correct - Choose The Response You Feel Is Most Important To Remember

Date ___ / ___ / ___ : S M T W Th F S

I feel:
(please circle)

because   because   because   because   because
_____   _____   _____   _____   _____
_____   _____   _____

Today I Am Grateful For

1. _____
2. _____
3. _____

What could help transform today into a remarkable day?

Reflective Writing

What have you learned about yourself in the process of accepting yourself and your life experience?

_____

_____

_____

_____

_____

_____

_____

How does self-acceptance differ from self-esteem?

a) Self-acceptance is based on external validation, while self-esteem is based on internal validation

b) Self-acceptance is about embracing all aspects of yourself, while self-esteem is about promoting a positive self-image

c) Self-acceptance is a constant state, while self-esteem can fluctuate

d) Self-acceptance is necessary for self-esteem, but not vice versa

All Are Correct - Choose The Response You Feel Is Most Important To Remember

Date ___/___/___: S M T W Th F S

I feel:
(please circle)

because   because   because   because   because

___   ___   ___   ___   ___

___   ___   ___   ___   ___

Today I Am Grateful For

1. _____

2. _____

3. _____

What could help transform today into a remarkable day?

Reflective Writing

What strategies have you used to become more accepting of yourself and your life experience?

_____

_____

_____

_____

_____

_____

_____

Which of the following is a sign that someone is struggling with self-acceptance?

a) Constant self-criticism and negative self-talk
b) Lack of motivation and drive
c) Difficulty setting and achieving personal goals
d) Avoidance of challenging situations

All Are Correct - Choose The Response You Feel Is Most Important To Remember

Date ___ / ___ / ___ : S M T W Th F S

I feel:
(please circle)

because _____ because _____ because _____ because _____ because _____

Today I Am Grateful For
1. _____
2. _____
3. _____

What could help transform today into a remarkable day?

Reflective Writing
How has accepting yourself and your life experience made you a better person?

_____

_____

_____

_____

_____

_____

_____

Why is it important to accept both the positive and negative aspects of yourself?

a) To maintain a balanced self-image
b) To avoid challenging yourself and taking risks
c) To please others and gain their acceptance
d) To gain a better understanding of yourself and your behaviors

All Are Correct - Choose The Response You Feel Is Most Important To Remember

Date ___ / ___ / ___ : S   M   T   W   Th   F   S

I feel:
(please circle)

because _____   because _____   because _____   because _____   because _____

Today I Am Grateful For

1. _____
2. _____
3. _____

What could help transform today into a remarkable day?

Reflective Writing

In what ways did you struggle with accepting yourself and your life experience?

_____

_____

_____

_____

_____

_____

_____

_____

Which of the following is a helpful strategy for practicing self-compassion and self-acceptance?

a) Comparing yourself to others
b) Setting unrealistic expectations for yourself
c) Practicing gratitude and self-forgiveness
d) Ignoring your feelings and thoughts

All Are Correct - Choose The Response You Feel Is Most Important To Remember

Date ___ / ___ / ___ : S   M   T   W   Th   F   S

I feel:
(please circle)

because _____ _____   because _____ _____   because _____ _____   because _____ _____   because _____ _____

Today I Am Grateful For

1. _____
2. _____
3. _____

What could help transform today into a remarkable day?

Reflective Writing

How did you become aware of the areas of your life that needed to be accepted?

_____

_____

_____

_____

_____

_____

_____

_____

Which of the following is an example of self-acceptance?

a) Believing you are perfect and have no room for improvement
b) Constantly criticizing and berating yourself for your mistakes
c) Embracing your quirks and unique qualities
d) Striving for perfection and avoiding failure at all costs

All Are Correct - Choose The Response You Feel Is Most Important To Remember

I feel:
(please circle)

because   because   because   because   because

_____ _____ _____ _____ _____

Today I Am Grateful For

1. _____
2. _____
3. _____

What could help transform today into a remarkable day?

Reflective Writing

How has accepting yourself and your life experience impacted your relationship with others?

_____

_____

_____

_____

_____

_____

_____

_____

How can challenging societal norms and expectations help with self-acceptance?

a) By promoting comparison and competition with others
b) By eliminating the need for self-reflection and introspection
c) By allowing for individuality and authenticity
d) By reinforcing the idea of a "perfect" and "flawless" self

All Are Correct - Choose The Response You Feel Is Most Important To Remember

Date ___ / ___ / ___ : S   M   T   W   Th   F   S

I feel:
(please circle)

because   because   because   because   because

_____   _____   _____   _____   _____

_____   _____   _____   _____   _____

Today I Am Grateful For

1. _____
2. _____
3. _____

What could help transform today into a remarkable day?

Reflective Writing

What moments during the process of learning to accept yourself and your life experience have been most meaningful to you?

_____

_____

_____

_____

_____

_____

_____

Which of the following is not a part of the self-acceptance process?

a) Recognizing and accepting your past experiences and mistakes
b) Seeking validation and approval from others
c) Taking responsibility for your actions and behaviors
d) Embracing your unique qualities and strengths

All Are Correct - Choose The Response You Feel Is Most Important To Remember

Date ___ / ___ / ___: S M T W Th F S

I feel:
(please circle)

because   because   because   because   because
_____ _____ _____ _____ _____
_____ _____ _____ _____ _____

Today I Am Grateful For

1. _____
2. _____
3. _____

What could help transform today into a remarkable day?

Reflective Writing

How has learning to accept yourself and your life experience helped you to be a more confident individual?

_____

_____

_____

_____

_____

_____

_____

How can mindfulness practice aid in self-acceptance?

a) By encouraging avoidance of difficult emotions and thoughts
b) By promoting self-criticism and comparison to others
c) By allowing for non-judgmental observation of one's thoughts and feelings
d) By reinforcing perfectionistic tendencies

All Are Correct - Choose The Response You Feel Is Most Important To Remember

Date ___ / ___ / ___ : S   M   T   W   Th   F   S

I feel:
(please circle)

because   because   because   because   because

_____ _____ _____ _____ _____

_____ _____ _____ _____ _____

Today I Am Grateful For

1. _____
2. _____
3. _____

What could help transform today into a remarkable day?

Reflective Writing

What advice would you give to someone who is struggling to accept themselves and their life experience?

_____

_____

_____

_____

_____

_____

_____

How does self-acceptance impact relationships with others?

a) It can lead to isolation and avoidance of social interactions
b) It can improve communication and connection with others
c) It has no effect on relationships with others
d) It can create jealousy and competition with others

All Are Correct - Choose The Response You Feel Is Most Important To Remember

Date ___ / ___ / ___ : S   M   T   W   Th   F   S

I feel:
(please circle)

because   because   because   because   because

_____   _____   _____   _____   _____

_____   _____   _____   _____   _____

Today I Am Grateful For

1. _____
2. _____
3. _____

What could help transform today into a remarkable day?

Reflective Writing

Describe the process of learning to accept yourself
and your life experience in three words?

_____

_____

_____

_____

_____

_____

_____

Which of the following is a common barrier to self-acceptance?

a) Fear of failure and making mistakes
b) Ignoring feedback and constructive criticism
c) Lack of self-awareness and introspection
d) Seeking external validation and approval

All Are Correct - Choose The Response You Feel Is Most Important To Remember

Date ___ / ___ / ___ : S   M   T   W   Th   F   S

I feel:
(please circle)

because   because   because   because   because

_____ _____ _____ _____ _____

_____ _____ _____ _____ _____

Today I Am Grateful For

1. _____

2. _____

3. _____

What could help transform today into a remarkable day?

Reflective Writing
How has the acceptance of yourself and your life
experience allowed you to grow as a person?

_____

_____

_____

_____

_____

_____

_____

_____

How can journaling help with self-acceptance?

a) By encouraging constant self-criticism and analysis
b) By promoting a distorted self-image
c) By providing a safe space for self-expression and reflection
d) By reinforcing negative thought patterns and self-perception

All Are Correct - Choose The Response You Feel Is Most Important To Remember

Date ___ / ___ / ___ : S M T W Th F S

I feel:
(please circle)

because   because   because   because   because
_____   _____   _____   _____   _____
_____   _____   _____   _____   _____

Today I Am Grateful For

1. _____
2. _____
3. _____

What could help transform today into a remarkable day?

Reflective Writing

What is the most valuable lesson you have learned in the process of learning to accept yourself and your life experience?

_____

_____

_____

_____

_____

_____

_____

_____

Why is it important to focus on the present moment when practicing self-acceptance?

a) To avoid dealing with difficult emotions and past experiences
b) To maintain a positive and optimistic outlook on life
c) To recognize and acknowledge current feelings and experiences
d) To distract from any negative thoughts and emotions

All Are Correct - Choose The Response You Feel Is Most Important To Remember

Date ___/___/___: S   M   T   W   Th   F   S

I feel:
(please circle)

because   because   because   because   because
_____ _____ _____ _____ _____
_____ _____ _____ _____ _____

Today I Am Grateful For

1. _____
2. _____
3. _____

What could help transform today into a remarkable day?

Reflective Writing

What emotions have you experienced while learning to accept yourself and your life experience?

_____

_____

_____

_____

_____

_____

_____

What is the first step towards self-acceptance?

a) Seeking validation and approval from others
b) Identifying and changing flaws and weaknesses
c) Embracing your strengths and unique qualities
d) Comparing yourself to unrealistic standards and expectations

All Are Correct - Choose The Response You Feel Is Most Important To Remember

Date ___ / ___ / ___ : S M T W Th F S

I feel:
(please circle)

because   because   because   because   because

_____ _____ _____ _____ _____

_____ _____ _____ _____ _____

Today I Am Grateful For

1. _____

2. _____

3. _____

What could help transform today into a remarkable day?

Reflective Writing

How has learning to accept yourself and your life
experience helped you to overcome challenges?

_____

_____

_____

_____

_____

_____

_____

_____

How can therapy help with the process of self-acceptance?

a) By providing a quick fix for self-esteem issues
b) By avoiding difficult topics and emotions
c) By offering a non-judgmental and supportive space for self-exploration
d) By promoting self-criticism and negative self-talk

All Are Correct - Choose The Response You Feel Is Most Important To Remember

As we reach the final pages of this journey through "Positive Mindset," I want to extend my heartfelt thanks to you. Your commitment to exploring positivity and its transformative power is not only commendable but a testament to your desire for personal growth and a richer, more fulfilling life experience.

Remember, the journey towards a positive mindset is ongoing and ever-evolving. Each day presents new opportunities to apply these principles, to learn, and to grow. I encourage you to revisit these pages whenever you need a reminder of your incredible potential to foster positivity and resilience in the face of life's challenges.

As we part ways, I leave you with a quote that has been a guiding star in my journey: "The greatest discovery of any generation is that a human can alter his life by altering his attitude."

– William James.

Thank you for allowing me to be a part of your journey. May your path be filled with light, hope, and endless possibilities. Farewell, and may you carry the spirit of positivity with you, today and always.

With gratitude and best wishes,

Sensei Paul David

Reflective Writing

_____

_____

_____

_____

_____

_____

_____

_____

_____

_____

_____

_____

_____

_____

_____

_____

_____

_____

_____

_____

The End

As you close the pages of this mindfulness journal, remember that each word you've written is a step on your journey towards self-awareness and inner peace. Embrace the moments of clarity, the revelations, and even the uncertainties you've encountered along the way. Let this journal be a testament to your growth and a reminder that every day offers a new opportunity to be present, to observe, and to appreciate the simple wonders of life. Carry these lessons forward, and may your path be filled with mindful moments and serene reflections. Until we meet again in these pages, be gentle with yourself and stay anchored in the now.

Mindfulness isn't difficult, we just need to remember to do it.

Thank You!

If you found this book helpful, I would be grateful if you would **post an honest review on Amazon** so this book can reach other supportive readers like you!

All you need to do is digitally flip to the back and leave your review. Or visit amazon.com/author/senseipauldavid click the correct book cover and click on the blue link next to the yellow stars that say, "customer reviews."

As always...
It's a great day to be alive!

Get/Share Your FREE SSD Mental Health Chronicles at
www.senseiselfdevelopment.care

Check Out The SSD Chronicles
Series CLICK HERE

Get/Share Your FREE All-Ages Mental Health eBook Now at

www.senseiselfdevelopment.com

Or CLICK HERE

senseiselfdevelopment.com

Click Another Book In The SSD BOOK SERIES:

senseipublishing.com/SSD_SERIES

CLICK HERE

Join Our Publishing Journey!

If you would like to receive FREE BOOKS, please visit **www.senseipublishing.com**. Join our newsletter by entering your email address in the pop-up box

Follow Sensei Paul David on Amazon

CLICK THE LOGO BELOW

FREE BONUS!!!
Experience Over 25 FREE Engaging Guided Meditations!

Prized Skills & Practices for Adults & Kids. Help Restore Deep-Sleep, Lower Stress, Improve Posture, Navigate Uncertainty & More.

Download the Free Insight Timer App and click the link below:
http://insig.ht/sensei_paul

About Sensei Publishing

Sensei Publishing commits itself to helping people of all ages transform into better versions of themselves by providing high-quality and research-based self-development books with an emphasis on mental health and guided meditations. Sensei Publishing offers well-written e-books, audiobooks, paperbacks and online courses that simplify complicated but practical topics in line with its mission to inspire people towards positive transformation.

It's a great day to be alive!

About the Author

I create simple & transformative eBooks & Guided Meditations for Adults & Children proven to help navigate uncertainty, solve niche problems & bring families closer together.

I'm a former finance project manager, private pilot, jiu-jitsu instructor, musician & former University of Toronto Fitness Trainer. I prefer a science-based approach to focus on these & other areas in my life to stay humble & hungry to evolve. I hope you enjoy my work and I'd love to hear your feedback.

- It's a great day to be alive!

Sensei Paul David

Scan & Follow/Like/Subscribe: Facebook, Instagram,
YouTube: @senseipublishing

Scan using your phone/iPad camera for Social Media
Visit us at www.senseipublishing.com and sign up for our
newsletter to learn more about our exciting books and to
experience our FREE Guided Meditations for Kids & Adults.